Reflections

of My Moody Moods

Harsimran Kaur

Made with ❤ on the BookLeaf Publishing Platform
www.bookleafpub.in
www.bookleafpub.com

Dedication

Our existence is but Poetry!

My poetry is dedicated to life and death, and everything in between!.

The joys, the sorrows, the triumphs, the defeats, the ups the downs, the known, the unknown.......the questions, the answers, the love, the betrayal, the beliefs, the doubts......just about everything!

Preface

"Reflections... of my moody moods" is a journey through the labyrinth of my emotions, a testament to the complexities and contradictions that make us who we are. Within these pages, I invite you to immerse yourself in the ebbs and flows of life, to navigate the twists and turns that shape our experiences.

These poems are born from the depths of my own soul, a reflection of the turmoil and tranquility that I've encountered on my own path. From the whispers of love and loss, to the cries of joy and despair, these poems traverse the vast expanse of my feelings. They are an exploration of the spaces between life and death, where the beauty and brutality of existence converge.

As you read these words, I hope you'll find yourself reflected in their lines, your own emotions and experiences resonating with the rhythms and rhymes. May these poems be a mirror to inspire you to reflect on your own moody moods, your own journey through the ups and downs of life.

Welcome to "Reflections... of my moody moods".

Acknowledgements

I am deeply grateful to many individuals.

Most of all to the two most important people in my life and also my biggest critics, my spouse and my son, without whom this collection of poems would not have been possible. They have been my rock, my inspiration, and my safe haven, I thank you for your unwavering love and encouragement. Your presence in my life has shaped the words on these pages in ways you may never know.

I would also like to express my gratitude to all my family and friends, for giving me myriad experiences in my life. Their contributions have enriched this collection beyond measure.

To my fellow poets and writers, who have inspired me with their words, their passion, and their dedication to the craft, I thank you for showing me the power of language to touch, to heal, and to transform.

And to the readers, who have picked up this book and are willing to embark on this journey with me, I thank you for your trust, your curiosity, and your love for words.

Thank you.

1. The Mysterious Heart

Silently, Oh ever so silently
Beating ever so incessantly
Tucked away is a tiny little piece d'art
I think people call it the heart!

Must have made the creator ponder
Over what he designed as the nature's wonder
Could become the biggest destroyer of mental peace?
And He thought he'd made a masterpiece!

Pumping blood through its spout
Tirelessly toiling day in and day out
How does it then get the time
To be involved in emotional slime?

In its soft folds
An eternity it holds!
In its warmth it envelops
All emotions that it develops!

In its entwining dark alleys
You can sense the depth of oceans and valleys,
The expanse of an entire universe,
And surprises that spring when a forest you traverse!

More dramatic than the drama of life
Scarier than the darkness of night
More intriguing than the suspense of death
More mysterious than the mystery of breath

Is the piece d'art
Very fondly called heart!
Be it love, hatred, compassion or pity
Revenge, care, fear or sympathy

When it comes to emotions, all laws it defies
Goes against the tide and logic it denies!
Nature's mysteries may be easier to unravel
But a heart's terrain is impossible to travel!

It can conquer storms and have the world at its feet!
But can't hold up against a beloved's heart and
Is sure to face defeat!!!!
Such is the beauty of this piece d'art!
It's so lovingly called Heart!!!!!!!!!!

2. Mother 'O' Mother

At the time she conceives
A tiny little seed
She has no inclination
For the life she would lead

Nurturing in her womb
A life by Lord's ordinance
For nine long months
She is an epitome of endurance

Brings forth into the world
A special unique child
The sheer joy of which
Makes the pain mild

Then she spends sleepless nights
Tending to the child's needs
With every chuckle she laughs
And with every tear her heart bleeds

Mother...
Raises little angels
Into independent adults
With every milestone they achieve
Her soul exults

Nursing injured knees,
Broken hearts and hurt egos
With amazing ease she handles
At every stage her child's woes

Over indulgent at times
And at times a little strict
She knows the art of benevolence
And knows when to restrict

Her love as pure as a pearl
Is so selflessly divine
Sans jealousy she basks in glory
Of her children when they shine

Mother....
Gives a shoulder to cry
When the tide's against you
Gives a hug so loving
When you are feeling blue

Even the deepest of wounds
Her kiss can heal
Her love is such a treasure
That no one can steal

The world may write you off
And your assets may be few
But you know she'll always be there
For nothing can shake her belief in you

God could not be everywhere
So he gave a mother in our life
Her love, her blessings forever
Would be etched in our heart's archive!

3. A Prayer

A prayer..... an urge, a sudden need
Seems to have arisen
I have a prayer to offer
Would anybody up there listen?
For it's rare that my hands go up
Coz you see I do not pray too often

I pray, Oh Lord! Please give me ignorance
The kind we literates lack
Ruining true spirit with logic and reason
Wealth of knowledge we stack
Please help me unlearn some lessons
Please take some unworthy teachings back

Please give me an attitude
But one that's fresh and positive
A winning attitude to win hearts
And the power to easily forgive
Please take away some selfishness and greed
And fill in me the desire to give

Please give me power
To see with more than my two eyes
Give me the vision to see beyond
The power to reach the skies
High not with the worldly possessions
But elevate my soul and make my spirit rise

Please give me the ability to laugh
Not on others but over life's little joys
To laugh away my worries and problems
To face whole gamut of experiences with poise
Please give me bliss and contentment, not euphoria
For I don't want to just momentarily rejoice

I pray, Oh Lord! Please give me childlike innocence
Without malice, without pretense
Let me not just be a sheep in the herd
Bless me with the ability to make a difference

Please keep me grounded with some humility
Like a deep rooted fruit laden tree
And yet like a bird in flight
Please let my spirit be free
I have a prayer...............

4. Children Of A Lesser God

As I pulled to a stop my car at a traffic light
A face showed up at the window, pathetic was its plight

The unkempt look made me cringe
I looked at the face with disdain
My diamond studded fingers shooed him away
But then suddenly, I felt ashamed and so vain

For staring at me with innocent eyes
Was a child begging for alms
His hair dirty and nose running
Hands barely reaching me with outstretched arms

He shrugged and move to another car
Put off by my reaction
But did manage to stir somewhere
My inner wisdom and emotion

You find them dime a dozen
On the streets everyday

And how we loathe them
And keep them from our children away

Not even a thought is spared
When we see little hands slogging
At times as domestic helps
Or being ordered around for serving

So often a bunch, all dirty and in tatters
Is seen hovering around in markets
Pouncing on a coin tossed or
Digging out leftovers from thrown packets

Thrown by the sometimes over fed
Clad in designer wear, pampered kids
Sulking over not getting a toy of choice
Taking for granted dear God's gifts

Yet strangely enough the street urchins
Often called children of a lesser God
Find joy in playing with sand and pebbles
For they don't have a Barbie or an i-pod

Oh the children of a lesser God
To poor parents you were born
Not by choice but default
Then why do we treat you with such scorn?

Oh the children of a lesser God
Your smile and your innocence
Is no different from the fortunate ones
Then where is your childhood, why its absence?

Oh the children of a lesser God
It's we who deserve the contempt
For failing in our duties towards you
For not even making an attempt

Oh the children of a lesser God
...................please forgive us!!

5. A Hug

A hug, an embrace,
a gesture so loving
A hug, an embrace,
shows you are caring

A hug, an embrace is only but an action
But depending on the situation
It conveys a different emotion!!

It's easy to decipher what a hug connotes
The way it's given, you know what it denotes!

A big warm hug can tell you 'Don't worry'
And then there's a hug that says 'I'm sorry'!!

Some hugs assure you 'Things are gonna be fine'
And some convey 'Better luck next time'

A sad tight hug to a dear one who's parting
Or a thumpy hug to one, after long you are meeting

A grateful hug can say 'Thank you'
As a comforting one says 'I'm there for you'!!

And always divine is a mother's hug
That makes a child feel so snug

Ever so protective is a hug from a father
That assures a scared child not to bother

A hug to express that you are sad or elated
A hug is the best way to be congratulated!

A lover's hug is so romantic and cozy
In your mind conjures a hundred pictures so rosy!!

A hug, an embrace
Can express feelings intense and help you say
What at times a thousand words may fail to convey!!

So go out and hug your dear ones around
Resolve conflicts and let happiness surround

For a hug, a loving embrace, is the best gesture
The ability to hug is a gift from nature!!

6. Gameplan

Here today, gone tomorrow!
Now laughter, now sorrow!!
'His' gameplan never ceases to amaze.
'He' confuses you, leaving you in a daze!

One moment celebrations transcend.
Next moment gloom and sadness descend.
In this vast ocean of human insanity
It's a funny balancing act of Divinity!

I understand the need to acknowledge
Acknowledge that power up there.
How would we learn to appreciate
If there was all love and no despair??

Only darkness helps value light
Hope gives us the courage to fight
Pain, agony, sorrow, grief
Their existence is all so brief!

When a loved one is forever lost
You crave to get them back at any cost
Bidding tearful adieu, your heart aches
Your faith in your dear god shakes!

But the beauty lies in the way time heals
The pain diminishes and the agony recedes
Tears are replaced by fond memories
Framed to be kept on mantelpiece!

Life conquers death, happiness prevails
Though the memories leave their trails
We move on with a new resilience
With a new promise, new brilliance!!

7. Fireplace

Sitting cozily with a cup of steaming coffee
In front of the fireplace
Staring into the crackling fire
Feeling the heat on my face

Watching the logs of wood burning
Giving warmth and a radiant glow
Exuberant sparks flying around
Behold! Did I see dead white ash below??

The logs, the fire
The sparks, the ash
The typical story
I thought in a flash

Our heart would have been
But a log of wood
Had the sparks of emotions
Not set it ablaze, as only they could!

The heat, the radiance of its fire
Has given birth to many a love story
But why after the fiery romance
The end of all sagas is so gory??

In fact it's true in all relations, all bonds
It seems everyone is out there to cheat
Back stabbing and hypocrisy is rampant
So is betrayal, contempt and deceit

Betrayal in family, betrayal at work
Betrayal in friendship, betrayal in love
Loss of trust and a scar so deep
Is all you get for yourself to keep

Reducing you to a mass of insecurities
What good was the fire with momentary heat??
Painful ashes are all that is left
Your beautiful heart actually forgets how to beat!!

Sitting cozily with a cup of steaming coffee
In front of the fireplace
Staring into the crackling fire
Feeling the heat on my face
I admire the glow, the warmth, the radiance
Yet I cannot help but dread the consequence!!

8. Suffocating Suffocation

A bird flutters her wings
Desperately in a cage
Please let me be free
It calls out in a rage

Stifled and helpless
Captivity makes it feel
If only she could fly
Would her wounds heal

Her soul prays
On the verge of renunciation
To get rid of the
Suffocating suffocation

Let the bird free
If it comes back, its yours
If it doesn't
It never was!

When the situations that bind you turn suffocating
......it's time to let go
When the people who are around you become
suffocating
.......it's time to let go
When the love that surrounds you gets suffocating
........it's time to let go

Let go....of the shackles that bite into your soul
Let go....of the constraints which keep you from your
goal
Let go....of the emotions in life which have no role

Let go........of all that is restricting
Let go........of all that is suffocating
Let go

9. Intoxicated

All that is galactic
All that is cosmic
Is apparently intoxicated
Seems to be inebriated

Spinning incessantly around the sun
For an impossible unison
Unmindful of the futility
The earth will revolve till eternity

Spreading its royal plume
As soon as dark clouds loom
Tipsy goes the peacock
And dances with gay abandon

Every soul I see around
Doesn't fail to astound

Intoxicated are the swaying trees
Under the influence of gentle breeze

You can actually feel a river's radiance
Flowing lovingly towards the confluence

Who in this wide world is not under intoxication?
Drenched in power and wealth
Some ostentatious, some stealth
Obsessed with beauty some girls uncouth
Or soaked in shallow pride, misled youth
An unassuming simpleton or one full of intellect
In each, signs of intoxication reflect

And then there is intoxication of love….
Love of a parent for a child
Or love for the nature wild
Love for the God up there
Or love for the one you care

Love in any form is intoxicating
Love in any form is inebriating

It fuddles your mind, it's heady for sure
It's an intoxication, but makes a soul pure
Forbiddance only fuels it more
The more you guzzle, the more it'll lure

Yes! I am in a state of intoxication
I am in a state of inebriation

10. It Pains

It pains me ……. to see people unhappy
unhappy not just with their own woes,
but unhappier with the happiness of their foes;
obsessed with 'This is mine' and 'I have more',
they are filled with jealousy to the core.

It pains me a lot………to see people fight
fight over issues so petty, with no relevance…
at times over relations, at times over inheritance;
wasting lives trying to possess, possess all things
materialistic,
running a mad race, on pretext of being futuristic.

It pains me………to see inflated egos
egos that ruin families and cause bloodshed;
causing road rages and communal hatred;
egos that ride stronger and higher than any force,
filled with pride, but no guilt, no remorse.

It pains me immensely....... to see humanity dying
dying a slow death are relations, all bonds of love are
fake;
ruthlessly we use others selfishly for our sake.
no compassion, no pity but certainly many disparities;
there's definite ulterior motive even behind most
charities.

I wonder what will be the fate....
of the overblown egos,
of the over stocked possessions;
of the high headedness,
of the enviable positions??

When the soul will leave the body;
Your condition would be Oh! so shoddy!
Neither your riches nor your ego
Would change your fate during last rites
Under the logs, you'll be on fire
Or beneath the soil, eaten by the mites!

So live a better life....
a life which gives joy,
joy to all those around you;
earn in terms of friendship and love
that treasure would be true;

borrow some innocence from a child
and learn from him to forgive;
for if we learn to live like children,
to the world, there would be so much to give!

It pains me ...... to see people growing!
It pains me........to see the world decaying!

11. Kaleidoscope

A dear friend says lovingly
Take all adversities sportingly
Keep smiling whatever comes your way
For life is too short to cry and waste away

But if you analyze the situation
We've been blessed with a myriad of emotions
And I feel all feelings one must feel
Both when sailing's smooth and when we get a raw deal

For you see.....there's
One body and one soul of a kind
One heart and just one mind
And yet emotions so many
I rather find it a little uncanny!!

Just as a rainbow would not have been so
Even if a single colour from it would go
Life would be colourless without the emotions' palette
Like a platter of spiceless food unappealing to the palate

How dull would life have been
If it was all goodness and no sin!
A smile wouldn't have been so dear
If it hadn't been for a tear!

Love would have never got its due
Had hate not made it worth its value!
Jealousy helps you appreciate tolerance
Just as disrespect highlights reverence!

If you've never sunken into sadness
You can never experience real happiness!
It's a kaleidoscope out there, an amazing array
Enjoy each hue, but in a balanced way

Emotions are the ingredients for a perfect life's recipe
Despite their rigmarole under heart's canopy!
So have a positive attitude for everything
.........and be happy!

12. Bubbly Dreamz

O my dancing dreamy bubbles
You're so amazingly beautiful
Just a little effort
And I get bountiful!

You're so similar to my dreamz
To my perception of this paranormal world
So very pure, so breathtakingly gorgeous
To me you're like treasured pots of gold

I can see a dozen rainbows in you
Like a crazy riot of colours so vibrant
Delicately floating, bumping, gliding flirtatiously
Whispering softly and yet so jubilant

My dancing bubbles you're just like my dreamz
Stunningly exquisite and yet so transient
Very colourful, very perfect, yet momentary
Reminding me always that nothing is permanent

A little coldness, a little hurt
Is all it takes for dreamz to shatter
And just but an ungentle touch
Bursts the bubbles and the rainbows scatter

My sweet delicate bubbles
Why are you like my dreamz?

13. Awake

I feel stronger today
More in control
In control of my life
In control of my emotions
I've broken the shackles of fear
Of all the emotional bonds
I cannot be a weakling
A victim of manipulations
I choose to live with pride
With my head held high
I refuse to be walked all over
Treat me like a doormat? Don't dare
I value my dignity finally
More than your selfish support
I'm no longer afraid to be alone
Walk out on me, I don't care!!
Or one day I'll walk away
Walk away to freedom
Freedom of my spirit
Freedom of my soul

I no longer desire acceptance
I no longer wish to please you all
No walls, no falls
No obligations, No expectations
I choose to rebel against all
And strangely it gives me strength
For today.........
I'm emboldened
I'm empowered
I'm awake

14. I saw God!

My narrative may seem odd
But I think I did see God!
Or I must have felt His presence
For so captivating was the ambience

No, I wasn't a pilgrim on a trip
Visiting man made faux places of worship
My encounter with Him was a chance
And I instantly fell into a trance

It wasn't a planned search by the way
I discovered Him while on a holiday!!
The seemingly ever elusive power of such stature
Was omni present right in the lap of the nature!

Far away....
Snow covered peaks looked glorious to the eye
Standing tall and majestic against the blue sky

And closer by....
Soft white clouds were playing hide and seek
Hugging and kissing the mountains on their cheek

There were oak and cedar forests all around
And through them a narrow serpentine road wound

White mist had enveloped the atmosphere
Like a possessed soul, my arms went up in the air
The cool crisp breeze was playing with emotion
Waking the Zorba in me, I danced with devotion

Devotion to God I could sense in all that was there
It was divine, it heavenly, an answer to my prayer!
To add to the magic, it began to drizzle
My soul exulted, there was nothing to grizzle

To escape the drizzle a herd of sheep huddled under a
tree
Oh! Such a picture perfect sight is a rarity!

Their shepherd was no less charismatic
For in his eyes was a gleam so hypnotic
I could've mistaken him for Krishna with those eyes
I'm sure the Gods belonged to such lands and not to the
skies

When so meditative was the environment
How could I not believe that God was present??

Of His omnipresence, this was just a sample
Go out, explore, the beautiful nature is His temple

I had always been accused of being an atheist
But I don't deny God, I'm a plain pantheist
For I believe firmly that God is nature and nature is God
And I am so ecstatic, cause Yes! I saw God!

15. I'm in Love

One day someone asked me
Are you in love?

I pondered for a while,
For I was not too sure
'Cause I really did not know
The true meaning of being in love!

Yet I confess that
My heart leaps with joy
When I bask in the shining sun
Or feel the rain against my face
Let the gentle breeze caress my hair
Or walk on the sands, leaving my trace!

Yes! I think I'm in love......with LIFE!

I see romance in....
Smiling at someone I do not know
Walking through the puddles on the road

Soaking in the beauty of flowers abound
I see romance in...........
Every little thing that I see around!

Yes! I'm sure I'm in love ....with LIFE!!

I look at nature and
The glorious mountains beckon me
Standing in their majestic splendour
The fragrance of pines, the gushing rivers
The sounds of birds, make me wonder

How could someone not fall in love??
There's love and music
In every creation of God
You just need to sense it
I'm sure you too will be awed!

Yes! I'm very much in love with a beauty called LIFE!!!

16. I am Unique

I know I am unique
I am God's creation

But.....I wonder how was nature created
I wonder then why it degenerated

I hear the symphony of nature's songs
I hear too the cacophony of mortals around

I see the expanse of His glory
I see too the deeds gory

I want to soak in the divine intoxication
I also want to detox my being from toxic potion

I pretend I am part of the beauty
I pretend too that the muck around is not for me

I feel all, that is true, pure, divine
I also feel the pain, the suffering, the decline

I touch the soft, velvety, feathery petals of life
I touch too the hard prickly thorns of strife

I worry I may lose my paradise
I also worry that fool may conquer wise

I cry with joy for every blessing
I cry too when I see pain and suffering

I understand every morning comes with a ray
I understand too that night follows day

I say there's hope in every moment
I say too that many a moment is a torment

I dream of love, laughter, happiness
I dream too of hate, gloom, sadness

I try to strike a balance
I try to keep up the pretense
That...
I am unique!

17. Smile

Two soft pink lips
A blessing only for the human race
Carrying out a score of tasks
They sure perk up the face

Eating, speaking, kissing et al
How for granted we take them always
Yet when you sit and ponder awhile
Their power will not cease to amaze!!

The seemingly insignificant pair
When decides to just ever so slightly curve
Out comes a smile
Causing many a heart to swerve

A smile costs you nothing
And doesn't need any resources great
Yet it is a curve that ironically
Can set many problems straight!!

So smile...
Smile a lot....
To your dear ones
Or to people you know
Smile without restrictions
Even to strangers you meet on the go!!

A smile can say
More than words at times
A smile can light up
The darkness in lives

A smile can diffuse
Situations out of control
A smile can help you
Win hearts and enthrall

But behold......
A smile when turns
Into a smirk or a sneer
Can cause damage irreparable
Or break the heart of someone dear!!

Never smile out of pleasure sadistic
Never over another's pain
If it is not straight from a loving heart
It'll reflect, no matter how you feign!!

18. Romance

There seems to be romance in the air
It has enveloped all that is there
From now to eternity
From finite to infinity

The flirtatious clouds, some dark,
some white and fluffy
Are romancing the splendid hills
Hugging them, kissing them softly
As if teasing lovingly before
Surrendering to their naughty wills

Showering on them their rains
Of warmth and love
Pouring down to be one as hand in glove
Softening even the most rigid
Melting even the most frigid

The gentle breeze is playing with emotions too
Sneaks up from behind like your beloved would do

Touches ever so lovingly, yes it knows the art
Conveying a hundred messages
Straight from your lover's heart

The freshly bathed leaves are bright but blushing
Reminiscing the way rain drops with them
were romancing
Insects and birds are also singing with exultation
Not a soul seems to have escaped the intoxication

My love says the mood is set for romance
I couldn't agree more, I'm in a trance
Oh God! Let no soul be deprived of love today
Coz to live, you give but only one chance!

19. Disillusioned

Love is a mirage.......
.... alluring
.... beckoning
.... promising
.... irresistible
In the burning hot desert of life
Conjures up an oasis in your mind
You run up to the delusion
Starry eyed you reach out
Only to realize it was intangible
Leave alone quenching your thirst
It drains you, leaves you parched

Love is a myth......
.... powerful
.... enduring
.... timeless
....but a myth
Boasting of eternity
Claiming to be celestial

It has entangled many
In a mushy quagmire
But mythical, as it is
It leaves you groping in the dark

Love is an illusion.........
...fascinating
....unbelievable
....deceptive
...conniving
....deceitful
Far from reality
It creates an image bizarre
On dawn of realization
You feel shattered, bruised, scarred
Irreparable, inconsolable, rife with skepticism
It leaves you utterly disillusioned

20. Emptiness

It's a strange feeling
An uncanny, eerie feeling
A feeling of restlessness
An undefined emptiness

A knock, a signal out of the blue
That everything is not okay around you!
A knock so untimely, a signal so scary
Just when life seems so perfect, far from dreary!

And then....I'm alone in the midst of a crowd
oblivious to the madness around
shocked and confused my mind reels
emptiness is all my heart feels

One moment a state of sheer bliss
Next there seems an eclipse
Sinking me in bottomless depths of despair
Imprisoning me in dungeons of fear

Despair.......over a dream unfulfilled or a hungry desire
Fear ....of losing someone or being used by one you
admire

The murkiness around blurs the vision of my wisdom
For opportunism is rampant and sincerity is seen seldom

Murky are the people, murkier are the games they play
Oh God! Give me the power to read selfish minds, I pray

My id, ego and superego...
the usually happy inmates of my conscience
squabble over such sporadic occurrence
though normally in a mode of acceptance
they begin to wobble between His defiance and
deference

Then comes along someone once in a while
Restores my faith in life and makes me smile
Fills my heart with blissful happiness
Then why again this knock?
....this fear of emptiness?

21. Permanence vs Transience

This mystery called life
It's so amazing
Our existence, our encounters
Leave so many questions blazing

Forever worried about tomorrow,
We ruin our today
Forever wanting to grab
Whatever comes our way

Forever obsessed with a fear
A fear of loss or decay
Fear of an eerie darkness
Fearing that night follows day

But why?
Why is joy short lived?
Why does every meeting end in a parting?
Why does every flower die away wilting?

Why after the playful youth is the old age agony?
Why does death overcome the beautiful journey?
Why does sorrow surface amidst laughter?
Why is there a lull, and a storm thereafter?

Emerges an astonishing butterfly
From the warmth and security of a cocoon!
But did the caterpillar transform
Only to perish so soon?

The today and tomorrow
Day and night
Life and death
Wrong and right
Ups and downs
Smiles and tears
The sun, the rain
And all those fears.....

Midst this madness of transience
Isnn't there anything permanent?
Something that could be assuring
That doesn't change, is constant?

Watch closely..........
Observe carefully...............
There's order in the chaos

The upheavals are all organized
There's perfect balance and harmony
To give us solace when we are agonized

In this truly amazing world
Only two things are constant and stable
One is the changes brought by nature
And one is true love that's most reliable!

22. Life and death

Here today, gone tomorrow!
Now laughter, now sorrow!!

'His' gameplan never ceases to amaze.
'He' confuses you, leaving you in a daze!

One moment celebrations transcend.
Next moment gloom and sadness descend.

In this vast ocean of human insanity
It's a funny balancing act of Divinity!

I understand the need to acknowledge,
acknowledge that power up there.
How would we learn to appreciate,
if there was all love and no despair??

Only darkness helps value light
Hope gives us the courage to fight

Pain, agony, sorrow, grief
Their existence is all so brief!

When a loved one is forever lost
You crave to get him back at any cost

Bidding tearful adieu, your heart aches
Your faith in your dear god shakes!

But the beauty lies in the way time heals
The pain diminishes and the agony recedes
Tears are replaced by fond memories
Framed to be kept on mantelpiece!

Life conquers death, happiness prevails
Though the memories leave their trails

We move on with a new resilience
With a new promise, new brilliance!!

23. A Match to Catch

Just another day
In his hectic life
Office was over
He had to rush home
Errands to run
Before he could 'catch the match'

Snarling traffic
Mad rush
And then this goddamn jam!!
Again some accident, he was told
A young lady, very critical
Could he help???
Police...... hospital.......
Too much hassle...........
Who has the time??
And then this match!!

Poor girl, he thought
I wish her family knows

And he drove back home
''Honey going to Mom's place, will be back by 8''
Read the sticker on the fridge
But it was now pretty late!!

The doorbell rang
''Ah! She's there''
.......A cop??
And that's her driving license he has!!
''Sir, that your wife??
Sorry! She is no more...
There was an accident
She could've been saved
But no one had time to spare.............!!''

24. Lost Spark

She was so full of life
Her heart was filled with laughter
Living each day as it came
Not a care about the before and after

Like a free spirited bird
She wanted to fly
With a song in her heart
She was on a different high

She smiled at the flowers
And played with butterflies
She danced in the rain
And romanced the clouds in the skies

She was so full of life
Her heat was filled with laughter
But then something changed her
And she forgot to live thereafter

Feeling trapped in her body
Now her soul is crying
She wants to live.....like before
But her heart is dying

She's desperate
To look for a reason to smile
It frustrates
When she can't find one worthwhile

The bottomlessness
Of this state is scary
Of losing herself,
Her sanity, she's wary

Oh Lord!
Restore her faith in love again
Let not her belief in fairy tales go vain
Can she still wish upon the shooting star at night?
Will there be, in shining armour, a knight?

Oh Lord!
She was full of life
Her heart was filled with laughter
She's losing that spark
Will she stay happily ever after?????

25. World of Make-Believe

I live in a beauteous world
My private little wondrous world

My world is a paradise
Filled with eternal bliss
Fragrant like a garden of roses
Where love would never go amiss

My world is devoid of pain
The kind malevolent people inflict
And it's not bereft of hope
For there's peace, no conflict

I live in a beauteous world
A world of make-believe
Call it a loss of perspective
If that's the way you perceive!

You live in the 'real' world
A world with all but 'reality'!

With abundant pain and hypocrisy
You must be proud of your practicality!

Peep into my world, or walk in
To be a part of my paradise
But please leave it alone
If all you can do is criticize

Too harsh for my soul
Is your 'real', your 'reality'
Yes, I do distance myself
From the 'practical', the 'practicality'!

Let me live in my little world
Please let me be
My world gives me solace
Here my spirit feels free

I do no harm to nobody
Then why am I asked to leave
My little beauteous world
My world of make-believe?

26. My Eyes

My eyes, they say, are dreamy and sad

Is it because of a paradise lost
Or maybe not found ?
Is it hurt, pain or a scar
Or grief profound ?
Or is it an unfulfilled dream
Or disillusionment with those around?

It makes me wonder!!
There are dreams for sure!
Childlike fantasies, insane but pure!
And in the ocean of sanity
Pearls in the oyster allure!

Am I nurturing a spirit that's out of sync?
Are the pearls illusive and desires surreal?
I'm scared and try to be stoic.
Convinced that my dreams are trivial.

Then there's sadness too, unexplained

One moment I'm assertive, completely in control
Next I crave assurance in embrace of strong arms!
Now I'm rejoicing with real people
And now I drift into solitude seeking calm!

Life has taught me lessons though!
I've learnt over the years the subtle difference
Between holding hands and chaining a soul to ours!
I've learnt that sunshine burns
If you get too much of it for hours!
I've learnt to plant my own garden
And not wait for someone to get me flowers!

See I've learnt to be realistic
I've learnt to live in this world!

But is it my fault
If my inner wisdom makes my soul yearn
To unlearn all that I've learnt??

The world of my dreams may be unreal
But it's so beautiful,
Without malice, pretense and contradiction
My resilient springy spirit strongly believes
In my distant dreams with child like conviction!!

27. The Ocean

I sat gazing at ....
the vastness, the expanse!
the beauty, the romance!

I stared into nothingness, at the never ending water
around!
In its bosom, it was nurturing, a different world, so
profound!

I watched the crabs being washed ashore
Running around on the rocks galore

Far away was an outline of a ship
Carrying hopes of many to reach home after a trip!

Picking up shells was such a pleasure!
Collecting all shapes, as if it were a treasure!

Some carefree happy fishermen were singing aloud
Spreading their net, to me it seemed like fishes' shroud!

The sun was slowly going down the horizon
Spreading a divine orange glow on the ocean!

The waves gently caressed my feet
And with them slid the sand beneath!

Why under my feet, the feel of slipping sand
Felt like time slipping out of my hand??

I stood gazing at the ocean......
It seemed so intriguingly eternal!
And my existence so fractional!

I stood contemplating on its moods so various!
Seemingly peaceful now, could get so unpredictably
furious??

The calm rhythm of the waves, as if breathing
Gently rising, approaching and then receding!

And yet, but an unrest down under
Could devastate and leave cities asunder!!

I was utterly confused with my paradoxical approach
I was awe-inspired, yet the reproach??

The romance, the beauty not withstanding
It's power to devour, I was apprehending!!

Pushing back all negativity
With a fresh mind I admired its magnanimity!!

And I felt music and rhythm in the seas
Like thousand resonating symphonies!!

I sat gazing
At life's mysteries!!
I sat laughing
At my unfounded worries!!
I sat enjoying
Life's bounties!!!

I sat gazing
At the expanse!!
I sat gazing
At the romance...........................

28. Don't Just Exist

You get but only one life
One life to live
You get but only one life
Don't just exist

In your eyes
Let your dreams be alive
Follow your heart
For your passion, strive

Feel each moment
Like the first breath
Feel each moment
As if follows death

Keep alive the child within
Keep fanning the desires there in
Don't stop living before you die
Don't let life just go by

Love someone like
There's no tomorrow
Hold on to the joys,
Let go of sorrow

Be quick to forgive
And quicker to forget
For there is a sunrise
After every sunset

Rise, rise and shine
No matter how often you fall
Try, try and try till you succeed
Show resilience like the spider on the wall

Don't let any pain rule
Life is too short to cry away
Go search for happiness
Out there is an impressive array

You get but only one life
One life to live
You get but only one life
Don't just exist

29. Slow Down

The bugging alarms
The race against time
The maddening pace
For everything sublime

The honking horns
The unforgiving road rage
The mad rush always
We've surely come of age!!

Forever in a tearing hurry
To meet some deadline or other
We miss out on the little joys
That the life has to offer!!

Ever paused for a moment to wonder
How romantic the moon looks every night?
And how many of us really miss it
On nights when it goes out of sight??

Ever slowed down to count and appreciate
The fresh leaves on your plants?
Ever admired the butterflies on flowers
Or any of the life's grants??

In a crazy pursuit of a bright tomorrow
Just don't miss out on the blessings today.
Like the small milestones your child achieves
Or the sweet nothings your spouse has to say!!

It really won't harm to slow down
Once in a while in this roller coaster life
Slow down for a conversation
To talk to your inner self, torn by strife!

Take a break in the lap of nature
There's no better healer around
The flowers, the clouds, the streams, the birds,
The rain, the sunshine.....there's beauty abound!!

No need to give up the worldly pleasures
For an experience of eternal bliss and joy
Just learn to see with more than your two eyes
And the subtle art of never letting an opportunity go by!!

--

30. Stolen Moments

I want to steal some moments,
Some moments of indulgence
Indulgence in small acts of pleasure,
Pleasure with that elusive essence

I want to steal a few moments
Just to stare into nothingness
To be with myself, my inner self
And yet not even feel the loneliness!

I want to steal some precious moments
From the maddening race
Just to enjoy the cool crisp breeze
To liven up my saddening face

I want to take out some moments
And take off my worldly mask
So I could drench in the rain
Or in the sun I could bask!

I can spend hours in admiration....
of the singing birds and swaying trees
of the amazing flowers and buzzing bees
of the faraway hills and their crowning clouds
of their serene quietness away from the crowds

I can spend countless hours
listening to the sound of untiring waves
revering an ocean's mystique, perplexed over how it
behaves

I wish I could spend endless hours
looking up in the sky
tying to find figures in the clouds
or simply watching them float by

I can spend hours and hours
But all I desire is a few stolen moments.............

A few precious stolen moments
To indulge in my stupid little pleasures..............
of walking barefoot in the grass
of touching every flower that I pass
of listening to the pitter patter of raindrops
of stepping out in puddles in my flip flops
of watching children play on the street
of enjoying unlimited tea, putting up my feet

of losing myself in an engrossing piece of literature
a thriller, a romantic or a take on nature
of enjoying soulful music of all genres
of cleaning cobwebs from my soul's corners...

I can spend hours and hours
But all I desire is a few stolen moments...............

31. Love

When there's music in the air
Like a thousand symphonies
When there's harmony and celebration
In melodious musical fantasies
When there's poetry in everything
In people, in flowers, in trees
When your exuberant soul
Exults and goes into ecstasies

Beware......... you're in love with life!

When summers seem like monsoons
And there's freshness all around
You hear the pitter patter of raindrops
And feel a nip even with sunshine abound
When rainbows replace mirages
And sights of frogs and mushrooms astound

Enjoy...............you're in love with life!!

When there's laughter in your heart
And soft murmurs unexplained
When there's a delectable fragrance around
And a feel of some celestial pleasures attained
When you're always over the moon as if
Your enthralling childhood you've regained
When you let go of your soul
And free your spirit that was restrained

Bask.......you're in love with life!!!

32. Woman of Substance

I am a woman
And I am proud to be one
Years of oppression notwithstanding
Against adversities I have won

Dominated at every step
Yet I learnt to live with pride
Used as an object or treated as a doormat
I took it all in my stride

I learnt to hold my head high
And fight my own fights
When the 'Man lost his spine'
I had to stand up for my rights

Where are you 'The man of nobility'?
Your pride, 'The man of courage', is at stake!!
Where are you, 'The warrior, the prince'??
Were all your virtues so frivolous, so fake????

Look at me...........
I am ogled at
Poked
Probed
Raped
Taken for granted every single day!!

My self esteem
My self respect
Takes a beating forever
But I don't get 'Cowed'.........Nay!!!

I do not dig for sympathy
By crying 'Victim of circumstance'
I advocate what is RIGHT
I am a ''WOMAN OF SUBSTANCE''

33. I Don't Like Aubergines

I presumed I was like an aubergine
Royal in appearance
A crown on the head
An air of superiority, surrounding me always
As if I was the most well bred!

I was but, just an aubergine
Who couldn't take any pressure
Cut and expose, it would blacken
Roast and it charred beyond recognition
Cook and it would get mushy
Losing its very identity

What was I doing to myself?

And I became a potato!
Boiled in adversities,
I managed to put up a brave front
But my vulnerable inside bore the brunt!

Why shouldn't I be like an egg?
Mostly happy with my sunny side up
Try to boil, and I go hard and tough!

And then I learned a lesson
The best lesson of my life……..

Brewing in the carafe
Was my humble morning coffee
Facing the adversity
To me, which was always catastrophe

But behold!
It did not succumb to pressure

Not losing its identity
When faced with an unfavourable condition
It made the most of situation
And gave an astounding rendition!

So now I've learnt to be like coffee beans
Goodbye eggs, potatoes and aubergines!!

34. My Moody Moon

He is like the moon
Forever changing
At times waxing
At times waning

Every night I see the moon
And admire its new phase
Coz it's like my beloved
Surprising me each day in different ways

One day, he is like the Full Moon
Calm and serene, yet shining bright
Bathing me in his smothering love
Like the earth on a moonlit night

But just when I am over the moon
For all the adoration I receive
The moon changes its mood
And it slowly begins to recede

I longingly look up in the sky
But the moon is oblivious to my plight
For it just keeps waning by
Slowly disappearing from my sight

And then there are nights
That are lonely and dark
For my moody moon goes missing
Leaving me wondering where's the spark?

But I know,
Full moon or New Moon or stages in-between
No matter what the phases are
I know the moon is always there causing the tides in my
heart

I am sure,
Whether visible or not
It's loving me all along
I understand it wanes
Only to come back strong